TOOLS OF THE TRADE

Tools of the Trade

POEMS FOR NEW DOCTORS

EDITED BY
Dr Lesley Morrison GP
Dr John Gillies GP and Chair, RCGP Scotland
Revd Ali Newell
Lilias Fraser

SCOTTISH POETRY LIBRARY

By leaves we live

First published in 2014 by
Scottish Poetry Library
5 Crichton's Close
Edinburgh
EH8 8DT
www.scottishpoetrylibrary.org.uk

ISBN 978-0-9562191-6-9

The publisher is grateful for all the donations towards the costs
of this anthology.

Typeset in Stone Print and Carter Sans by Gerry Cambridge
gerry.cambridge@btinternet.com
Produced by Productive Production, www.productive.uk.com
Printed and bound in Scotland

CONTENTS

FOREWORD

CONGRATULATIONS ON graduating as a doctor. We offer you this little book of poetry, *Tools of the Trade*, as a friend to provide comfort and support as you begin your work. Some poems are sad, some are funny, all cast light on the experience of being a doctor. Some of you may love poetry, some may not have discovered it, others may think that it's not for you. We challenge you not to find something in these pages that connects with your emotions and feelings. Being a doctor is a privilege; it is also very demanding and can be stressful, and to be able to look after others, we need to look after ourselves. Sharing your concerns, talking with colleagues, writing and listening can help alleviate your stress. There are others willing to listen and to help. The BMA has a confidential counselling service and university chaplaincies offer confidential support. Growing interest in the helpful insights that literature can offer is evidenced also by Kenneth Calman's *A Doctor's Line: Poems and Prescription in Health and Healing* (Sandstone Press, 2014) which uses texts from the literature of Scotland over the last 700 years to comment on health, social issues and medicine. To help others to attain health, we need to preserve and nourish our own physical, mental, emotional and spiritual health.

We would like to thank Robyn Marsack, Lilias Fraser, Kay Bohan and the Scottish Poetry Library for their expertise and enthusiasm. We are grateful to all those, many of them doctors themselves, who generously donated funds for the project. The poets deserve our sincere thanks for creating the poems and for allowing us to publish them here. Ali Newell, Associate Chaplain at the Edinburgh University Chaplaincy, joined us for the enjoyable and very difficult task of reducing the list of possible poems to the selection that occupies these pages. Lesley, Pat Manson's widow, believed that the book was a fitting tribute to Pat and provided warm encouragement. We thank her for that.

And we thank Pat who inspired the book, and who would have been delighted to see it in print and to know that you new doctors are receiving it.

Enjoy it, carry it with you, share it with others. Let Robyn and Lilias know of any poems you especially like. Let them know of any that you think we could or should have included.

Use the poems as tools to connect with your patients, your colleagues, yourself.

Dr Lesley Morrison
GP

Dr John Gillies
Chair, RCGP Scotland

TOOLS OF THE TRADE *Martin MacIntyre*

New doctors will be empowered by poems
in the pockets of their metaphorical white coats.
There at the ready:
on early, sweaty, scratchy, ward rounds
to deploy while waiting patiently for the consultant's
   late appraisal;
give filing, phlebotomy and form-filling an edge
   and depth;
sweeten tea-breaks as if with juxtaposed Jaffa Cakes
to answer that persistent bleep—while sneaking a pee,
to travel the manic crash and flat-lined emptiness of
   cardiac arrest
thole the inevitability of the inevitable;
to pace with careful cadence;
stop and breathe usefully
arrive ready not to recite by rote;
to be alone with on the boisterous bus home
to txt anxious Mums and Dads—'Are you remembering
   to feed yourself?'
'YES. LOL. Smiley-face—perhaps a frog?'
to place strategically on the cup-ringed cabinet—first
   night on-call,

thrust under the sun-torn pillow on the morning
    following the first night on-call
find undisturbed, but at a different verse, following the
    jumpy party, following the first night on-call
to steal insights into the science of nurses' smiles
to prepare for change.
To take a full history, examine closely and reach a
    working diagnosis: 'You are a human being.'
      'The stars sing as whitely as the mountains.'
To investigate with prudence.
To reconsider the prognosis in the light of better-quality
    information.
To appreciate; pass on; ponder
challenge, relinquish,
allow, accept
be accosted by dignity.
To forgive and free.

A TIGHT-ROPE ACT   *Gael Turnbull*

Holding our breath
in apprehension,
we grasp life.

A MEDICAL EDUCATION *Glenn Colquhoun*

for Dr Peter Rothwell

In obstetrics I learnt that a woman opens swiftly like an
    elevator door.
The body wriggles free like people leaving an office on a wet
    afternoon.

In medicine I learnt that the body is the inside of a watch.
We hunch carefully over tables with blunt instruments.

In paediatrics I learnt that the body is a bird.
I leave small pieces of bread in fine trails.

In geriatrics I saw that the neck becomes the shape of an
    apple core.

In intensive care I discovered that the body is a number.
The sick sweat like schoolboys studying maths before a test.

In orthopaedics I found that the body can be broken.
Bones make angles under skin as though they were part of
    a collapsed tent.

In anaesthetics I saw people hang on narrow stalks like
ripe apples.

But in the delivery suite I learnt to swear.

I wrote the poems in Playing God *as a young doctor and so many
of my experiences in medicine were experiences I was having for
the first time. Human beings stood out differently in each specialty.
I felt as though I was bobbing from flowerbed to flowerbed in
some huge botanical garden. I was also encountering the body as
a character for the first time and learning that each part carried
its own personality and possibility of friendship. Often this was
distinct from the person it was part of.*

THE DOOR *Miroslav Holub*

Go and open the door.
  Maybe outside there's
  a tree, or a wood,
  a garden,
  or a magic city.

Go and open the door.
  Maybe a dog's rummaging.
  Maybe you'll see a face,
or an eye,
or the picture
  of a picture.

Go and open the door.
  If there's a fog
  it will clear.

Go and open the door.
  Even if there's only
  the darkness ticking,
  even if there's only
  the hollow wind,
  even if

       nothing
            is there,
go and open the door.

At least
there'll be
a draught.

THE GUEST HOUSE *Jelaluddin Rumi translated by Coleman Barks*

This being human is a guest house.
Every morning a new arrival.

A joy, a depression, a meanness,
some momentary awareness comes
as an unexpected visitor.

Welcome and entertain them all!
Even if they're a crowd of sorrows,
who violently sweep your house
empty of its furniture,
still, treat each guest honorably.
He may be clearing you out
for some new delight.

The dark thought, the shame, the malice,
meet them at the door laughing,
and invite them in.

Be grateful for whoever comes,
because each has been sent
as a guide from beyond.

From A LIFE FOR A LIFE *Dinah Craik*

Oh, the comfort—the inexpressible comfort of feeling *safe* with a person—having neither to weigh thoughts nor measure words, but pouring them all right out, just as they are, chaff and grain together; certain that a faithful hand will take and sift them, keep what is worth keeping, and then with the breath of kindness blow the rest away.

TENDER *Sarah Broom*

when I look around me
the world is very bright

it is so light and shiny
that my long bones shiver

I am not quite sure
that I have what it takes
to stay alive in this world

I need to stay very still
and let the air move past
and through me

I am tired and tender

when my limbs meet each other
crossing on my lap
I want to cry
with the pleasure
of resting them

when tears come
my bones turn to water

and I sleep

From A YEAR AND A DAY:
19 OCTOBER 1979–19 OCTOBER 1980
Gael Turnbull

To be taken in small doses as required

October

25: Miss G——, born while Queen Victoria was still alive, standing proudly in the middle of her sitting room in front of a blazing fire, big school-girl grin on her face: 'It's stomach trouble! I'm a terror for stomach trouble.'

November

19: Not yet thirty, her bones full of metastatic breast cancer, so painful she can't bear to be touched, and her two year old son can't understand why his mother won't let him hug her any more.

January

29: 'My husband is all crumbling up.'

30: 'Thank you for listening, doctor. I likes to unravel a bit.'

June

1: 'All blind inside my head if you take my meaning.'

4: Behind the Surgery car park, a blush of roses and on the
lawn, a milky way of daisies.

5: 'Threw a coat at him as there wasn't a saucepan handy.'

6: Hailstones in the sunshine, bouncing on the pavement
like pearls from a broken necklace.

15: 'If you want my considered judgement: he's pissed.'

October

1: 'My head is full of little men with needles and I feel like
one hundred and nine.'

2: His tie stiff with grease and traces of food and pinned to
his shirt with a safety pin... asking for 'something to make
me go, proper!'

12: Clouds like shreds of sheep wool stuck on a gorse bush, blown and bleached by the sun and the rain... then dabbed with scarlet and magenta.

14: In a little brown gnome hat, puffing and blowing, head almost completely sunk between his shoulders, helped along by a plum pudding wife... his mouth stretched in a permanent grin, one tooth showing.

Gael was a good listener and observer of detail—essential to both his writing and doctoring. His spur-of-the-moment decision to record something heard, seen, or experienced every day for a year brings to life the resilience, humour, sorrow and strength of his patients and the small delights of the seasons.

JILL TURNBULL

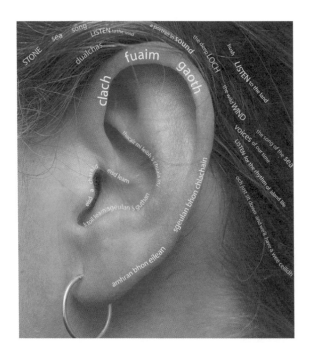

From **DOING CALLS ON THE OLD
PORTPATRICK ROAD**   *Iain Bamforth*

12. *Graham's Landing*
'The ear says more
Than any tongue'

I thought I spoke the language
asking what the matter was, the wrong.
I only wanted to know your history
framed in the window of our time.

Which of us should have first say?
One who inhaled the long firth,
one who seemed a slow-island-Joe,
one who clambered the bare scree up—

The house put on its afternoon disguise,
wrong way round and inside out.
Language was an unreliable hidey-hole
for two social beasts in harness:

me, losing track of the unreliable words
called bait and purchase, you
dangling them in the cold blue sound
that wandered past the window.

'Graham's Landing', part 12 of a thirty-poem sequence based on my year as trainee GP in Galloway in 1993, is a tribute both to an admired elder poet who lived (for) his poetry as completely as it was possible to do in the late 20th-century and a patient, who—it may well be suspected—is at least a hobby fisherman, word-shy but motive-sly. In fact, it's not clear whether doctor or patient is 'dangling' the hooked lines here. Both are harassed, somewhat awkward, possibly failing to recognise the other fully in the clinical encounter. I can recall my younger self twenty years ago looking out over a patient's shoulder through 'the window of our time' at the light effects on Luce Bay and recalling how W. S. Graham allows the sea to surge and swell in his lines—sometimes playful, invariably punning—in a way that is both compelling and mysterious.

The way technologies uncouple the senses has always intrigued me, not least by dint of the fact that technical acumen in medicine is now so overwhelmingly sighted (and occupies an ever increasing share of the 'clinical gaze') while the face-to-face of the clinical encounter is archaic, always allied to hearing: in this sense, language is closer to an odour or perfume, circulating beyond its origins in unforeseen and ungovernable ways. Religion and rhetoric are coupled to what the mouth says; in medicine, by contrast, attending properly to a patient reverses the power roles and allows Graham's witty phrase to develop its full meaning: 'the ear says more / Than any tongue.'

And the title is, after all, 'Graham's Landing': the hints dropped by feeling ('bait and purchase') do get taken up in spite of language's artful attempts to conceal its wants.

RECOVERY ROOM *Patricia Beer*

The noise in the recovery room
Was half footfall and half hum

Like a well-mannered gallery
Of pictures that I could not see.

And then a name disrupted it:
The hated name of childhood: Pat,

A name I had not answered to
For fifty years and would not now.

Another voice began to talk:
Pat. And still I did not speak.

My husband waited in my room
And in the end they sent for him,

After an hour or two of this.
I heard Patricia. And said 'Yes?'

NIGHT SISTER *Elizabeth Jennings*

How is it possible not to grow hard,
To build a shell around yourself when you
Have to watch so much pain, and hear it too?
Many you see are puzzled, wounded; few
Are cheerful long. How can you not be scarred?

To view a birth or death seems natural,
But these locked doors, these sudden shouts and tears
Graze all the peaceful skies. A world of fears
Like the ghost-haunting of the owl appears.
And yet you love that stillness and that call.

You have a memory for everyone;
None is anonymous and so you cure
What few with such compassion could endure.
I never met a calling quite so pure.
My fears are silenced by the things you've done.

We have grown cynical and often miss
The perfect thing. Embarrassment also
Convinces us we cannot dare to show
Our sickness. But you listen and we know
That you can meet us in our own distress.

A BRIEF FORMAT TO BE USED WHEN CONSULTING
WITH PATIENTS   *Glenn Colquhoun*

The patient will talk.

The doctor will talk.

The doctor will listen while
the patient is talking.

The patient will listen while
the doctor is talking.

The patient will think that the doctor
knows what the doctor is talking about.

The doctor will think that the patient
knows what the patient is talking about.

The patient will think that the doctor
knows what the patient is talking about.

The doctor will think that the patient
knows what the doctor is talking about.

The doctor will be sure.
The patient will be sure.

The patient will be sure.
The doctor will be sure.

Shouldn't hurt a bit, should it?

I love the consultation. It is the high altar of medicine, God and priest and man all in the same place at the same time, no-one knowing who is who and someone always roaming around. It strikes me how much is assumed within it and how most of the time those assumptions are accurate…most of the time.

'I FELT A CLEAVING IN MY MIND' *Emily Dickinson*

I felt a Cleaving in my Mind—
As if my Brain had split—
I tried to match it —Seam by Seam—
But could not make them fit.

The thought behind, I strove to join
Unto the thought before—
But Sequence ravelled out of Sound
Like Balls—upon a Floor.

AN SUAIMHNEAS BRUAILLEIN /
IN THE TRANQUILLITY OF DELIRIUM

Màrtainn Mac an t-Saoir

'S ann ri ur seanair Dòmhnall Buachaille
a bha sibh a' bruidhinn a-raoir
thuirt sibh rium.

Ann an aisling no an soillearachadh seòmair choimhich,
chomhairlich e dhuibh
eadar ceathramhan a chuid òran
gur ann car mar seo a bha i,
an t-slighe
eadar beatha is bàs
air uairean dorcha, ro dhorcha
aig àmannan eile gun dad ga dìth.

Bha sibh mar pheata dha
dh'inns e dhuibh
fear a dh' fhalbhadh le cuman cùramach gu tobar
    ghinealach
fear a dh'fhadadh blàths à cruaich a chridhe
fear a dh' èigheadh prìsean sa Bheurla air creutairean nach
    gabhadh creic

fear a chunntaiseadh na fàrdain chumhanga nam ficheadan:
notaichean mòra geala an Rìgh aig a' bhodach fo leab' a làithean.

Ach cha tug e freagairt idir
air coltas chùisean
an tùs an fhuarain?
an sùil nan lasraichean?
air an fhèill mhòir mhaireannaich
gun dròbhair no beathach no airgead no eagal?

Agus is math sin 's dòcha,
gu h-àraid, tha grèim ur làimhe deise ag agairt,
seach nach do dh'fhaighneachd sibh dheth.

¶

You were conversing last night
with your grandfather Dòmhnall Buachaille
you said to me.

In a dream or in the clarity of an alien ward,
he advised you
between verses of his songs
that it was a bit like this,
the journey
between life and death
sometimes dark, too dark
at other moments without imperfection.

You were like a pet for him
he told you,
someone who could run with a careful pail to the well
    of generations
someone who could kindle warmth from the stack of
    his heart
someone who could call prices in English for creatures
    that couldn't be sold
someone who'd count tight farthings into piles:
the King's large white notes under the old man's bed
    of days.

But he didn't give any kind of answer
about the look of things
at the source of the fount?
in the eye of the blaze?
at the great everlasting fayre
without drover or beast or money or fear?

And maybe that's just as well,
especially, the grip in your right hand contends,
since you didn't ask him.

*Thòisich mi an dàn seo air an trèan dhachaigh às A' Bhealach
an dèidh dhomh tadhal air m' athair nach maireann is e air stròc
a ghabhail.*

*I started this poem on the train home from Balloch, having just
visited my Dad in hospital. He'd recently suffered a stroke.*

THINGS *Fleur Adcock*

There are worse things than having behaved foolishly
    in public.
There are worse things than these miniature betrayals,
committed or endured or suspected; there are worse things
than not being able to sleep for thinking about them.
It is 5 a.m. All the worse things come stalking in
and stand icily about the bed looking worse and worse
    and worse.

INCREASINGLY SOPHISTICATED METHODS OF
DIVINATION USED IN THE PRACTICE OF MEDICINE

Glenn Colquhoun

By observing a rooster pecking grain.
By the various behaviours of birds.
By balancing a stone on a red-hot axe.
By the shape of molten wax dripped into water.

By observing a yellow flame on a burning candle.
By following the movements of mice.
By counting the number of moles on the body.
By examining the entrails of animals.

By the pattern of shadows cast onto plastic.
By the colour of paper dipped in urine.
By the growing of fresh mould in round dishes.
By the magnification of blood.

By the alignment of electricity around the outside of the heart.
By the rise in a column of mercury.
By timing exactly the formation of clots.
By the examination of excrement.

By the placement of sharp needles underneath the skin.
By tapping the knee with a hammer.
By the bouncing of sound against a full bladder.
By the interpretations of pus.

By the attractions of the body to strong magnets.
By the characteristics of sweat.
By listening carefully to the directions of blood.
By waiting to see what happens next.

*Studying the history of medicine always gives perspective to the
opinions and orthodoxies of the present. In my experience not
many people really know what they're doing. I think it is always
wise to believe and doubt in equal measure.*

From WILHELM MEISTERS LEHRJAHRE /
WILHELM MEISTER'S APPRENTICESHIP:
 'WHEN WE TAKE PEOPLE MERELY THE WAY
   THEY ARE...'
Johann Wolfgang Von Goethe, translated by Iain Bamforth

'Wenn wir die Menschen nur nehmen, wie sie sind, so
machen wir sie schlechter; wenn wir sie behandeln, als
wären sie, was sie sein sollten, so bringen wir sie dahin,
wohin sie zu bringen sind.'

'When we take people merely the way they are we make
them worse than they are; when we treat them as if they
were already what they should be, then we make them
everything they could be.'

'IN THIS SHORT LIFE' *Emily Dickinson*

In this short Life
That only lasts an hour
How much—how little—is
Within our power

From **ULTRASOUND**   *Kathleen Jamie*

for Duncan

i. *Ultrasound*

Oh whistle and I'll come to ye,
my lad, my wee shilpit ghost
summonsed from tomorrow.

Second sight,
a seer's mothy flicker,
an inner sprite:

this is what I see
with eyes closed;
a keek-aboot among secrets.

If Pandora
could have scanned
her dark box,

and kept it locked—
this ghoul's skull, punched eyes
is tiny Hope's,

hauled silver-quick
in a net of sound,
then, for pity's sake, lowered.

TWENTY-EIGHT WEEKS *Lesley Glaister*

We nearly missed her.
This little storm of life,
could have blown by
before we weathered her.
But here she is: sturdy,
definite, pointing her finger
for *this* and *this* and *more*
and more and more.

TEDDY *Glenn Colquhoun*

for a child with leukaemia

Teddy was not well.
Teddy had been feeling sick.
Teddy had to go to hospital.
Teddy was told that he had too much blood.
Teddy did not miss his friends.
Teddy knew the thermometer was not sharp.
Teddy was not scared of needles.
Teddy said the medicine would make him better.
Teddy closed his eyes at night.
Teddy ate his vegetables.

Teddy's small girl lay in the corner of his bed.
She was not so sure.
Her eyes were made from round buttons.
The fluff on the top of her head was worn
as though it had been chewed.

I wrote this poem for a three year old patient with leukaemia. She
screamed at her doctors whenever we entered her room on the ward.
On Christmas Day Santa Claus gave her a water pistol. After that

we were allowed in as long as we were shot one by one without mercy. She is well now and trains dogs. Water pistols should be a mainstay of cancer treatment.

ADAM, THERE ARE ANIMALS *Chloe Morrish*

There is a small fox
slipping through the fabric of morning,
still coated in a layer of grey dusk

and carefully placing his paws
between what's left of night
in the garden.

There is a monkey,
a stained toy, in your hand
when you arrive at the hospital,

which none of the fussing people
had noticed
and you had clung to.

There are wild-eyed soldiers' horses,
charging at us from the jigsaw pieces
in the waiting room

where we try to sleep
on the table and chairs
and pretend we're not waiting.

There are several pigeons
on the window ledge, shuffling about
before the steel chimneys and pinking sky

and a seagull's bark
in the deflated quiet
just after you die.

There is an overfed cat
in the arms of a nurse who smokes
by the automatic doors.

and there are baby rabbits
eating the grass verges
of the hospital car park.

There is our dog
at the door, confused
when we get home without you.

And on the kitchen table we sit at, dazed
and not quite real, with cups of tea to hold on to,
there is a small plastic horse.

'HE HAS ACHIEVED SUCCESS..'

Bessie Anderson Stanley

He has achieved success, who has lived well, laughed often, and loved much; who has gained the respect of intelligent men and the love of little children; who has filled his niche and accomplished his task, whether by an improved poppy, a perfect poem, or a rescued soul; who has never lacked appreciation of earth's beauty, or failed to express it; who has always looked for the best in others and given the best he had; whose life was an inspiration and whose memory a benediction.

THE BONNIE BROUKIT BAIRN *Hugh MacDiarmid*

Mars is braw in crammasy,
Venus in a green silk goun,
The auld mune shak's her gowden feathers,
Their starry talk's a wheen o' blethers,
Nane for thee a thochtie sparin',
Earth, thou bonnie broukit bairn!
—*But greet, an' in your tears ye'll droun*
The haill clanjamfrie!

crammasy	*crimson*
wheen o' blethers	*pack of nonsense*
broukit	*neglected*
haill clanjamfrie	*whole crowd of them*

THE OLD LADY   *Iain Crichton Smith*

Autumn, and the nights are darkening.
The old lady tells us of her past once more.
She muses on the days she spent nursing

at ten shillings a month. 'And what exams!
I could understand anything in those days.
What summers we had then, what lovely autumns.'

And so I imagine her cycling to her work
among the golden leaves, down avenues,
to hospitals which were disciplined and stark

with hard-faced matrons, doctors jovial
with an authority that was never quizzed,
while grizzled Death suckled at his phial,

and autumn glowed and died, outside the ward,
and girlishly she saw it fade in red
in sky and sheet, and evening was barred
with strange sweet clouds that hung above the bed.

HIS STILLNESS *Sharon Olds*

The doctor said to my father, 'You asked me
to tell you when nothing more could be done.
That's what I'm telling you now.' My father
sat quite still, as he always did,
especially not moving his eyes. I had thought
he would rave if he understood he would die,
wave his arms and cry out. He sat up,
thin, and clean, in his clean gown,
like a holy man. The doctor said,
'There are things we can do which might give you time,
but we cannot cure you.' My father said,
'Thank you.' And he sat, motionless, alone,
with the dignity of a foreign leader.
I sat beside him. This was my father.
He had known he was mortal. I had feared they would
    have to
tie him down. I had not remembered
he had always held still and kept quiet to bear things,
the liquor a way to keep still. I had not
known him. My father had dignity. At the
end of his life his life began
to wake in me.

MUM *Arthur Cochrane*

We sat together in silence.
The lost look in your eyes.
Once they were like eternal stars.

You were full of joy and love.
But now is pain and loneliness,
Lost in your own world.

You cry out *Mum*.
But she has been gone some
Twenty years.

You cry out *Mum*.
I pray for the kiss of death to come.
My love.

NOTHING *Selima Hill*

Because she is exhausted
and confused,

and doesn't want to argue,
and can't speak,

she dreams of nothing
for a thousand years,

or what the nurses cheerfully call
a week.

WARNING *Jenny Joseph*

When I am an old woman I shall wear purple
With a red hat which doesn't go, and doesn't suit me.
And I shall spend my pension on brandy and summer
   gloves
And satin sandals, and say we've no money for butter.
I shall sit down on the pavement when I'm tired
And gobble up samples in shops and press alarm bells
And run my stick along the public railings
And make up for the sobriety of my youth.
I shall go out in my slippers in the rain
And pick flowers in other people's gardens
And learn to spit.

You can wear terrible shirts and grow more fat
And eat three pounds of sausages at a go
Or only bread and pickle for a week
And hoard pens and pencils and beermats and things
   in boxes.

But now we must have clothes that keep us dry
And pay our rent and not swear in the street
And set a good example for the children.
We must have friends to dinner and read the papers.

But maybe I ought to practise a little now?
So people who know me are not too shocked and surprised
When suddenly I am old, and start to wear purple.

GOING WITHOUT SAYING   *Bernard O'Donoghue*

i.m. Joe Flynn

It is a great pity we don't know
When the dead are going to die
So that, over a last companionable
Drink, we could tell them
How much we liked them.

Happy the man who, dying, can
Place his hand on his heart and say:
'At least I didn't neglect to tell
The thrush how beautifully she sings.'

From *FINIS EXOPTATUS*   *Adam Lindsay Gordon*

Life is mostly froth and bubble,
Two things stand like stone,
Kindness in another's trouble,
Courage in your own.

FROM THE ROYAL COLLEGE OF SURGEONS
OF EDINBURGH *Andrew Greig*

My only talent lay in these.
My father rubbed his hands together,
stared as though their whorls held codes
of thirty years obstetric surgery.
It's manual craft—the rest's just memory
and application. The hard art
lies in knowing when to stop.

He curled his fingers, a safe-cracker
recalling a demanding lock;
I glimpse a thousand silent break-ins;
the scalpel's shining jemmy pops
a window in the body, then—quick!—
working in the dark remove or
re-arrange, then clean up, quit,
seal the entrance. Oh strange burglar
who leaves things better than he found them!
On good days it seemed my fingertips
could see through skin, and once inside
had little lamps attached, that showed
exactly how and where to go.

He felt most kin to plumbers, sparks and joiners,
men whose hands would speak for them.

I wander through the college, meet
portraits of those names he'd list,
Simpson, Lister, Wade and Bell,
the icons of his craft, recalled
as though he'd known them personally.
Impossible, of course. Fingers don't see.
Yet it gave me confidence, so I could proceed.

I stare at the college coat of arms,
that eye wide-open in the palm,
hear his long-dead voice, see again
those skilful hands that now are ash.
Working these words I feel him by me,
lighting up the branching pathways.
Impossible, of course, and yet it gives
me confidence. We need
to believe we are not working blind;
with his eye open in my mind
I open the notebook and proceed.

SECOND OPINION *Douglas Dunn*

We went to Leeds for a second opinion.
After her name was called,
I waited among the apparently well
And those with bandaged eyes and dark spectacles.

A heavy mother shuffled with bad feet
And a stick, a pad over one eye,
Leaving her children warned in their seats.
The minutes went by like a winter.

They called me in. What moment worse
Than that young doctor trying to explain?
'It's large and growing.' 'What is?' 'Malignancy.'
'Why *there*? She's an artist!'

He shrugged and said, 'Nobody knows.'
He warned me it might spread. 'Spread?'
My body ached to suffer like her twin
And touch the cure with lips and healing sesames.

No image, no straw to support me—nothing
To hear or see. No leaves rustling in sunlight.

Only the mind sliding against events
And the antiseptic whiff of destiny.

Professional anxiety—
His hand on my shoulder
Showing me to the door, a scent of soap,
Medical fingers, and his wedding ring.

TO MY SURGEON *Valerie Gillies*

No-one else sees me
drowning in the white wave
sprinkled with a terrible salt

invasive lobular carcinoma
is difficult to identify

but you take one look
and I am

held
by your hand
saving my life

THESE ARE THE HANDS   *Michael Rosen*

for the 60th anniversary of the NHS

These are the hands
That touch us first
Feel your head
Find the pulse
And make your bed.

These are the hands
That tap your back
Test the skin
Hold your arm
Wheel the bin
Change the bulb
Fix the drip
Pour the jug
Replace your hip.

These are the hands
That fill the bath
Mop the floor
Flick the switch
Soothe the sore
Burn the swabs

Give us a jab
Throw out sharps
Design the lab.

And these are the hands
That stop the leaks
Empty the pan
Wipe the pipes
Carry the can
Clamp the veins
Make the cast
Log the dose
And touch us last.

From **PLAYING GOD**   *Glenn Colquhoun*

10. A note of warning to patients when all else fails

Sometimes the needle is too blunt.
The stethoscope is too quiet.
The scalpel will not cut.
The scissors chew like old men's gums.

Sometimes the book has not been written.
The pill cannot be swallowed.
The crutches are too short.
The x-rays hide like dirty windows.

Sometimes the thermometer will not rise.
The plaster will not stick.
The stitches cannot hold.
The heart conducts a normal ECG.

Then I have to ask you what to do

Which is what you might
have wanted all along.

*There is a great deal of medicine that doctors possess not because
they have been to medical school but because they have lived life.
They have been sons and daughters and mothers and fathers
and friends and lovers. If they are lucky they will have failed,
with care around them to ease the fall. If they are unlucky they
will still be waiting to do so. Sometimes it is the medicine these
experiences teach us that is the most powerful of all. It can take a
long time to see this and sometimes a longer time to trust it.*

BEANNACHT / BLESSING   *John O'Donohue*

for Josie, my mother

On the day when
the weight deadens
on your shoulders
and you stumble,
may the clay dance
to balance you.

And when your eyes
freeze behind
the grey window
and the ghost of loss
gets in to you,
may a flock of colours,
indigo, red, green
and azure blue,
come to awaken in you
a meadow of delight.

When the canvas frays
in the currach of thought
and a stain of ocean

blackens beneath you,
may there come across the waters
a path of yellow moonlight
to bring you safely home.

May the nourishment of the earth be yours,
may the clarity of light be yours,
may the fluency of the ocean be yours,
may the protection of the ancestors be yours.

And so may a slow
wind work these words
of love around you,
an invisible cloak
to mind your life.

HUMAN CHAIN *Seamus Heaney*

for Terence Brown

Seeing the bags of meal passed hand to hand
In close-up by the aid workers, and soldiers
Firing over the mob, I was braced again

With a grip on two sack corners,
Two packed wads of grain I'd worked to lugs
To give me purchase, ready for the heave—

The eye-to-eye, one-two, one-two upswing
On to the trailer, then the stoop and drag and drain
Of the next lift. Nothing surpassed

That quick unburdening, backbreak's truest payback,
A letting go which will not come again.
Or it will, once. And for all.

From **OUR NATIONAL PARKS** *John Muir*

Climb the mountains and get their good tidings.
Nature's peace will flow into you as sunshine flows
into trees. The winds will blow their own freshness
into you, and the storms their energy, while cares will
drop off like autumn leaves.

WARD 64 *Sarah Broom*

the curtain's beige and orange checks
do nothing to divide us

when her drip beeps I think it's mine

when she hears the bad news
I have to put my iPod on to keep it out

across the room he's lost his wedding ring
because he's got so thin

skinny fingers
I'd better watch out for that

there is poetry all over the walls
of oncology

and I want to get out

From **CUMHA CHALUIM IAIN MHICGIL-EAIN /**
ELEGY FOR CALUM I. MACLEAN
Somhairle MacGill-Eain / Sorley MacLean

Tha an saoghal fhathast àlainn
ged nach eil thu ann.
Is labhar an Uibhist a' Ghàidhlig
ged tha thusa an Cnoc Hàllainn
is do bhial gun chainnt

The world is still beautiful
though you are not in it,
Gaelic is eloquent in Uist
though you are in Hallin Hill
and your mouth without speech

THE BIRD THAT WAS TRAPPED HAS FLOWN

James Robertson

in memoriam Vicky Patterson

The bird that was trapped has flown
The sky that was grey is blue
The bone that was dead has grown
The dream that was dreamed is true
The locked door has been swung wide
The prisoner has been set free
The lips that were sealed have cried
The eye that was blind can see
The tree that was bare is green
The room that was dull is bright
The sheet that was soiled is clean
The dawn that was dark is light
The road that was blocked has no end
The unknown journey is known
The heart that is hurt will mend
The bird that was trapped has flown

To every thing there is a season, and a time to every
purpose under the heaven:
A time to be born, and a time to die; a time to plant, and
a time to pluck up that which is planted;
A time to kill, and a time to heal; a time to break down,
and a time to build up;
A time to weep, and a time to laugh; a time to mourn, and
a time to dance;
A time to cast away stones, and a time to gather stones
together; a time to embrace, and a time to refrain
from embracing;
A time to get, and a time to lose; a time to keep, and a time
to cast away;
A time to rend, and a time to sew; a time to keep silence,
and a time to speak;
A time to love, and a time to hate; a time of war, and a
time of peace.

THE FLYTING O' LIFE AND DAITH *Hamish Henderson*

Quo life, the warld is mine.
The floo'ers and trees, they're a' my ain.
I am the day, and the sunshine
Quo life, the warld is mine.

Quo daith, the warld is mine.
Your lugs are deef, your een are blin
Your floo'ers maun dwine in my bitter win'
Quo daith, the warld is mine.

Quo life, the warld is mine.
I hae saft win's, an' healin' rain,
Aipples I hae, an' breid an' wine
Quo life, the warld is mine.

Quo daith, the warld is mine.
Whit sterts in dreid, gangs doon in pain
Bairns wantin' breid are makin' mane
Quo daith, the warld is mine.

Quo life, the warld is mine.
Your deidly wark, I ken it fine

There's maet on earth for ilka wean
Quo life, the warld is mine.

Quo daith, the warld is mine.
Your silly sheaves crine in my fire
My worm keeks in your barn and byre
Quo daith, the warld is mine.

Quo life, the warld is mine.
Dule on your een! Ae galliard hert
Can ban tae hell your blackest airt
Quo life, the warld is mine.

Quo daith, the warld is mine.
Your rantin' hert, in duddies braw,
He winna lowp my preeson wa'
Quo daith, the warld is mine.

Quo life, the warld is mine.
Though ye bigg preesons o' marble stane
Hert's luve ye cannae preeson in
Quo life, the world is mine.

Quo daith, the warld is mine.
I hae dug a grave, I hae dug it deep,
For war an' the pest will gar ye sleep.
Quo daith, the warld is mine.

Quo life, the warld is mine.
An open grave is a furrow syne.
Ye'll no keep my seed frae fa'in in.
Quo life, the warld is mine.

flyting	*disputation*
lugs	*ears*
maun dwine	*must fade*
maet	*food*
ilka wean	*each child*
crine	*shrivel*
dule	*misery*
ae galliard hert	*one gallant heart*
ban	*curse*
duddies braw	*glad rags*
lowp	*leap over*
bigg	*build*
gar	*make*
syne	*next, thereafter*

AT EIGHTY *Edwin Morgan*

Push the boat out, compañeros,
push the boat out, whatever the sea.
Who says we cannot guide ourselves
through the boiling reefs, black as they are,
the enemy of us all makes sure of it!
Mariners, keep good watch always
for that last passage of blue water
we have heard of and long to reach
(no matter if we cannot, no matter!)
in our eighty-year-old timbers
leaky and patched as they are but sweet
well seasoned with the scent of woods
long perished, serviceable still
in unarrested pungency
of salt and blistering sunlight. Out,
push it all out into the unknown!
Unknown is best, it beckons best,
like distant ships in mist, or bells
clanging ruthless from stormy buoys.

GIFT *Czesław Miłosz*

A day so happy.
Fog lifted early, I worked in the garden.
Hummingbirds were stopping over honeysuckle flowers.
There was no thing on earth I wanted to possess.
I knew no one worth my envying him.
Whatever evil I had suffered, I forgot.
To think that once I was the same man did not embarrass me.
In my body I felt no pain.
When straightening up, I saw the blue sea and sails.

From **DISENCHANTMENTS** *Douglas Dunn*

Mineral loneliness. The hour of stone.
A boat cut loose. Not much to steer it with.
Grey branches hanging over Acheron.

Look to the living, love them, and hold on.

PSALM EIGHTY-EIGHT BLUES *Diana Hendry*

Lord, when I'm speechless
when something—not just sorrow
but under that—a dull, numb, nameless dreich
about the heart I hardly seem to have,
when this afflicts me,
when hope's been cancelled,
when the pilot light of me's put out,
when every reflex and response
has been extinguished,

send word, snowdrop, child, light.

LINES FOR A BOOKMARK *Gael Turnbull*

You who read...
May you seek
As you look;
May you keep
What you need;
May you care
What you choose;
And know here
In this book
Something strange,
Something sure,
That will change
You and be yours.

ACKNOWLEDGEMENTS

Our thanks are due to the following authors, publishers
and estates who have generously given permission to
reproduce works:

Fleur Adcock, 'Things' from *Poems 1960–2000* (Bloodaxe
Books, 2000), by permission of the publisher; Patricia Beer,
'Recovery Room' from *Autumn* (Carcanet Press, 1997), by
permission of the publisher; Iain Bamforth, 'Graham's Landing' from *Open Workings* (Carcanet, 1996), by permission of
the publisher; Sarah Broom, 'tender', from *Gleam* (Auckland
University Press, 2013), by permission of Auckland University Press and Michael Gleissner; Sarah Broom, 'Ward 64',
from *Tigers at Awhitu* (OxfordPoets / Carcanet Press, 2010),
by permission of the publisher; Arthur Cochrane, 'Mum',
by permission of the author; Glenn Colquhoun, 'A medical
education', 'A brief format to be used when consulting with
patients', 'Increasingly sophisticated methods of divination
used in the practice of medicine', 'Teddy', and 'A note of
warning to patients when all else fails', all from *Playing God:
Poems about medicine* (Steele Roberts, 2002), by permission
of the publisher; Emily Dickinson, 'I felt a Cleaving in My
Mind' and 'In This Short Life', from *The Complete Poems
of Emily Dickinson*, ed Thomas H Johnson (Little, Brown,
1960) © President and Fellows of Harvard College; Douglas

Dunn, 'Second Opinion', from *Elegies* (Faber & Faber, 1985),
and 'Disenchantments', from *Dante's Drum-kit* (Faber &
Faber, 1993) by permission of the publisher; Valerie Gillies,
'To My Surgeon', from *The Hand That Sees: Poems for the
quincentenary of the Royal College of Surgeons of Edinburgh*
(Royal College of Surgeons of Edinburgh / Scottish Poetry
Library, 2005) by permission of the author; Lesley Glaister,
'Twenty-eight Weeks', by permission of the author; Goethe,
translated by Iain Bamforth, by permission of the translator;
W. S. Graham, from 'Private Poem to Norman MacLeod', by
permission of Rosalind Mudaliar, the Estate of W. S. Graham;
Andrew Greig, 'From the Royal College of Surgeons of Edinburgh', from *This Life, This Life: New and Selected Poems 1970-
2006* (Bloodaxe Books, 2006), by permission of the publisher;
Seamus Heaney, 'Human Chain', from *Human Chain* (Faber &
Faber, 2010), by permission of the publisher; Hamish Hend-
erson, 'The Flyting O' Life and Daith', from *Collected Poems
and Songs* (Curly Snake Publishing, 2000), by permission of
the author's Estate; Diana Hendry, 'Psalm Eighty-Eight Blues',
from *Twelve Lilts: Psalms & Responses* (Mariscat Press, 2003),
by permission of the author; Selima Hill, 'Nothing', from
Gloria: Selected Poems (Bloodaxe Books, 2008), by permission
of the publisher; Miroslav Holub, 'The Door', from *Poems
Before & After: Collected English Translations* (Bloodaxe Books,
2006), by permission of the publisher; Kathleen Jamie,
'Ultrasound', from *Jizzen* (Picador, 1999), by permission of

Pan Macmillan; Elizabeth Jennings, 'Night Sister', from *Collected Poems* ed Emma Mason (Carcanet Press Ltd, 1987), by permission of the publisher; Jenny Joseph, 'Warning', from *Selected Poems* (Bloodaxe, 1992), © Jenny Joseph, reproduced with permission of Johnson & Alcock Ltd; Màrtainn Mac an t-Saoir / Martin MacIntyre, 'Tools of the Trade', by permission of the author, and 'An Suaimhneas Bruaillein' / 'In the Tranquillity of Delirium' from *Dannsam led Fhaileas: Let Me Dance with Your Shadow* (Luath Press, 2006), by permission of the publisher; Hugh MacDiarmid, 'The Bonnie Broukit Bairn', from *Complete Poems, Vol I* ed Michael Grieve, W. R. Aitken (Carcanet Press Ltd, 1994) by permission of the publisher; Somhairle MacGill-Eain / Sorley MacLean, from 'Cumha Chaluim Iain MhicGil-Eain' / 'Elegy for Calum I. MacLean', from *O Choille gu Bearradh: Dain chruinnichte / From Wood to Ridge: Collected Poems* (Carcanet Press / Birlinn, 1999), by permission of Carcanet Press Ltd; déirdre ní mhathúna, 'Èisd / Listen', by permission of the author; Czesław Miłosz, 'Gift', from *New & Collected Poems 1931–2001* (Allen Lane, The Penguin Press, 2001) © Czesław Miłosz Royalties Inc, 1988, 1991, 1995, 2001, reproduced by permission of Penguin Books Ltd; Edwin Morgan, 'At Eighty', from *Cathures: New Poems 1997–2001* (Carcanet, 2002), by permission of the publisher; Chloe Morrish, 'Adam, There Are Animals', by permission of the author; Bernard O'Donoghue, 'Going Without Saying', from *Gunpowder* (Chatto, 1995), by permission of the author; John O'Donohue, 'Beannacht / Blessing', from *Echoes of Memory*

Errata

From **PRIVATE POEM TO NORMAN MACLEOD** *W. S. Graham*

The spaces in the poem are yours.
They are the place where you
Can enter as yourself alone
And think anything in.

NOTES